Resisting the Masquerade

RON GAVALIK

Pittsburgh Poet

First Edition

Published by Pittsburgh Poet
Pittsburgh, Pennsylvania
Author: Ron Gavalik
Proofreading and Editing: Rebecca Hoffman
Cover Illustration: Pittsburgh Poet Contributors

ISBN-13: 978-1-7320697-8-7

Experience more works by Ron Gavalik at
PittsburghPoet.com

For Nick and John,
the two boys who made me a man.
This one's for you.

Making it through life can be daunting. No matter the level of one's wealth or ingenuity, there is no escape from the bills, toxic lovers, bosses, and the long reach of villains. Confused and angry, one can easily abandon independent thought for the groupthink of tribal life. Rather than expose the soft underbelly in a free exploration of our world, it is far easier to adopt the ideologies of the mob. Insulated from enlightenment, a temporary and usually false sense of comfort can be found in winning the approval of others.

Over time, however, conformity wears on the mind and one begins to suffocate under the plastic resin of the masquerade. Truth can only be suppressed for so long. Eventually, the soul revolts in fits of violent resent, directed at others or at oneself.

Throughout my life, I've witnessed this kind of turmoil within myself and in the behaviors of those I encounter. I see it regularly on sidewalks and inside restaurants. In a society that celebrates the constant con, there are few moments when we tear away from the mob's claws. That act is perhaps the greatest form of moral dissent. That's also why I assembled the free verse in this collection. The works here are not solutions for the troubles of life, but rather raw perspectives, in which each of us can identify. Through the pursuit of truth, we can rise above the gutter, know the right questions, and then become the answers we need.

In creating Resisting the Masquerade, I give thanks to my editor and most trusted literary ally, Rebecca Hoffman. I also offer my utmost gratitude to the TRUE Readers who financially support my poetic endeavors. Without those beautiful souls, I simply cannot publish these works. Of that small band of subscribers, I raise my whiskey glass to **Steve Lipnichan**, my leading contributor and heroic supporter in Pittsburgh. Steve's ferocious support for the arts is why writers, painters, musicians, and others pursue our continued exploration of humanity. In short, I am grateful and humbled.

In these next pages, it's my aim that we tear down the walls that inhibit our path to enlightenment. We will then embark on a sightseeing tour that meanders through our lives and reminds each of us of our importance in this world. Thanks to my friend, Ron Sparks, who once described for me his torment of the masquerade and thus inspired the title of this collection, I prefer we take the time to think a little deeper and rediscover our power.

It's my position that many of us have lost our mettle, our fortitude, our ability to stand up to the grifters and shapeshifters that use our hearts as stepstools. Instead, we've donned masks of conformity and escape. When we rediscover the confidence to straighten our backs, the beauty buried inside each of us will then cascade as a rainstorm. Our power will wash away the soot that has polluted our spirits. As lovers and warriors, our hearts can then become the refuge for loved ones who seek peace.

—Ron Gavalik

"First they ignore you.
Then they ridicule you.
And then they attack you and want to burn you.
And then they build monuments to you."
–Nicholas Klein

The perilous life
is the rebellion
of human advancement
The safe life
is obedience

Most Intimate Perils

A man wakes every morning
and makes a choice.
Staring into the mirror, he decides
to participate or rebel or sin.

Swimming with the current
of the mob appears to be the path
of least resistance.

For the man whose spirit roars,
conformity is the ultimate sacrifice.
To commit such atrocities
against oneself
requires great courage.

Staring into his own eyes,
that man knows loathing.
He is intimate with the perils
of losing himself.

Under the Surface

The soul never sleeps
or dies or goes mad.
Those failings are reserved
for human casks,
average men and women
huddled in darkness.
We paint portraits and write truths
that reflect our troubles
on smartphones, bar napkins,
and in toilet stalls.

The soul does none of these things.
It just lives peacefully
under the surface and provides us
the much-needed fantasy
of better times that never come.
The fantasy keeps our lungs breathing
and makes sure the heartache
doesn't finish us off.

Organic Rebellion

In a Pittsburgh suburb,
I walked through an empty parking lot
near a department store
that had fallen out of public favor.
Blacktop covered the fertile ground
as a smooth, suppressive order
forced upon a wild Earth
that yearned to breathe free.

A single dandelion had sprouted
between the pores of the prison.
Weathered, barely clinging to life,
some of the flower's petals
appeared to give the world
its middle finger.

I gently picked the dandelion.
Careful to preserve its message,
I pressed it firmly between the pages
of a poetry journal I carried around.
The flower had been heard in life.
In death, its legacy would live on.

Inhale

I often have no clue
what words will come
when pouring blood
onto the page.
The soul has a life
and a will of its own.
Sins and truths, much like smoke,
live in the surrounding air.
They wait for someone
to inhale.

The Darkest Day

There are times I feel so alone,
worthless, useless, despised.
During these moments,
I'm never sure if I'll make it.
A piece of good news comes
that reminds me
full bottles of booze
and smiles from kind women,
they still exist. The sun rises
and clear skies still happen.
While I know in my bones
the darkest day is yet to come,
that day is in the future.
I still have my madness,
it surges through me
as the energy of life.

The Fight

Give me the fight,
the hard blows
between honest men
and determined women
who lust for that mad taste
of blood and cum.

The fight that blossoms
on behalf of struggle
is what I call beauty.
An old widow's thoughtful stare
is beauty. The worker's tireless
calls for solidarity is beauty.
A priest who chokes up
while delivering the last rites,
that's artful beauty.

The beauty of the fight
is a resurrection of the spirit
that can no longer remain dormant.
Without the fight,
there is no true love or true sex,
no appreciation for the stars,
nor is there a cosmos to explore.

For all the poetry written
about flowers, trees,
and ocean waves,
real beauty exists in the eyes
of the struggling soul.

The honored fight all their days
to breathe, feast, and pray

on their own terms,
and to die in peace.

Pavement View

I tripped and fell
onto the jagged sidewalk.
My palms and cheek burned
across the pavement.

After a moment, I sat up
and leaned against the wall.
There was no rush
to stand or walk
or even give a damn.
Responsibility awaited me
up there in the air.
Down on the pavement,
no one minds the bum.

I watched as a roach crawled
in the street toward the curb.
After a minute or two, that roach
made the impossible climb.
It too was on the run.

From the Ashes

There was once a fire
behind my rib cage.
The inferno crackled; it popped.
Its red flames pumped passion
through my mind and body.
On the coldest nights,
winter's demons surrounded us.
Outnumbered and outgunned,
the fire fought with courage
to hold off the frozen claws
that aimed to freeze my heart.

As the years passed into history,
the fire that raged inside of me
dwindled to embers.
Alone in a drafty house,
shivering, I considered the end.
Then the remaining coals whispered
in a raspy voice of an old soothsayer,
'The rest of the journey is up to you.'
A few swallows of whiskey later
and some determination,
I pressed onward
to the spring.

Modern Weeds

I'm trying <!DOCTYPE html>
<html> Baby, I'm trying <head>
<style>
div.container
background-color: #ffffff;
I'm trying <title> to see through
all the weeds <"width=device-width">
<style> of our modern landscape,
but I know my attempts {:left;background}
are futile efforts. {font-family:Arial, sans-serif}
{font-family:Georgia, serif} This is our world
now, and I'm just trying ;11px;font
</style>
to make it
</head>
through
<body>
the madness
</body>
of these weeds.

More to it all

I once tried to fly.
As I leapt from the tree,
the taste of the air
helped me realize
there was more to it all.
'Hey world!' I yelled.
'Get ready
for me!'

On the years-long descent,
fists of dried, cracked skin
and calloused fear
repeatedly beat me
down
in back alleys
upon cracked blacktop.

I tumbled through space
until I accepted
the security of the cage.

Sometimes at night,
I shimmy out
between the rusty bars.
The air tastes good,
I think,
because it goes on
and on
for a long time.

Know it not

Sometimes I try to add up
all the times I've died.
With each rebirth
comes knowledge, perspective.
The visual tint changes
from green to blue to gray.
Every time that shit happens
I feel like now I've finally got it all
figured out. Then I'm hit
with a confusing new reality,
and I'm reminded, I know
nothing. I suppose
that's alright.

...went on

The night went on
as the madness kept coming.
There was nothing
I could do
to stop it.
Eyes closed,
I prayed long and hard
for the dawn.

Humans Need

Humans need
less inspiration and more answers,
less hope and more truth,
less spectacle and more words,
less sex and more love.
We need to listen and understand,
drink water, eat good food,
laugh, kiss, and weep
until a long sleep.

Slithered Words

The best poem
came to me last night
while shaving.
I didn't write it down,
and now,
much like the shaving cream
that slithered down the drain,
those words are gone.

Exaggerated Acceptance

The rain clouds rolled
over the trees on the hillside.
Thunder boomed over the rivers.
Drunkards on the sidewalks
stumbled toward the next bar.
Women in sexy heels
trotted to shelter in all directions.
Children howled and laughed.
A hot, boring afternoon
would soon come to an end.

The mob's exaggerated reaction
to the slight change in weather
sparked anxiety. My heart raced.
Then I glimpsed the old man
on the corner. He leaned
against that same old telephone pole
and dragged on a cigarette.
The old man had seen it all:
war, murder, births, marriage, illness.
Retired from the feeding frenzy,
he casually observed life unfold.

I then halted my march to the apartment
and leaned against the building's wall.
Drops smacked the top of my head,
they rolled down my cheek.
The rain reminded me
that I am of the Earth,
and when the system is ready,
back to the Earth I will go.

Reasonable Paranoia

There is nowhere left to run
or blend into the crowd.
Surveillance cameras,
smartphones, the internet,
they expose our diseases.
In pursuit of ideals
decayed under a rusted sun,
the mob salivates and cries
for the total extermination
of those who live truth.
Drink up, baby.
Our time draws nigh.

privilege

I'm a whore
who sells himself
for the privilege of food.
Existing in your world
of surface beauty
and splendor,
that's the only payday
I've ever known.

Revenge Porn

It was a Wednesday night
in winter many years ago.
I stripped naked and stood
in front of the living room window
while listening closely to a pianist
interpret Bach on YouTube.
I wanted the neighbors
to call the cops
or gossip among themselves.
As the music streamed, I realized
a pronounced hatred for each of them
for living such boring lives.
My cock rested comfortably
on the wooden window ledge.
The texture felt sublime.
So I stood there on display
for half a concerto.

Times, Places, Reasons

The things that matter
depend on time and circumstance.
I've never met a man
who admitted to feeling horny
in morning traffic.
The bills don't exist
upon that first taste of air
after a day at the job.
No one goes unloved
seconds before the orgasm.
Most importantly,
nothing erases the onslaught
of invading cockroaches
faster than dim lighting,
that soft chair in the corner,
and bourbon with ginger ale
poured gracefully
over the tongue.

Slaughter Cometh

They had beat me down
a long time ago
in an alley of tar and stones.
I fought back, hard.
I held my own
until they slunk away,
back to the sewers
from where they came.

After more years pass,
they'll return for more.
Again, I will fight hard
for a while,
but with a diminished hunger,
a body slowed.
That's when they'll finally
have me.

When the pounding comes,
I plan to look up at the stars.
Blood and bones,
worries and women,
they'll soon vanish.
The sky will begin to spin.
My spirit, torn from its flesh,
will then explore the cosmos...
...so it goes.

Inured to it

The rust ran deep
under my fingernails.
At first, I worked at it
with the tip of a pocket knife.
A few scrapings broke loose,
but most of the rust remained.
I then scrubbed my hands raw
with soap and a brush over the sink.
Bits of skin peeled from my fingertips.
Again, the rust didn't budge.
Eventually, I gave up the struggle
and learned to accept the rust
as a permanent part of life.
After a while, I no longer saw rust
under my fingernails, but rather
a lifetime of experiences.
I saw rivers and streets,
history and buildings,
in this very special place
I will always call home.

Flame Dance

It was just past 2:00 am
on a lonely New Year's Eve.
I drove across the Rankin Bridge
and noticed a gold flame dance
atop a stack at the mill.
I stopped the car
in the middle of the bridge
and walked over to the rail.
In the darkness above the river,
the suffering didn't exist.
It would return
with the sun.

Be Villains

Creativity is to twirl
in colors within safe spaces
outlined by fragile curtains.
Art is to push against
and wear away the fabric,
to reveal new vistas.
The artists who grow dangerous
are denounced as heretics.
Artists who refuse to obey
are vilified and removed
from safety.

Stumble Beautifully

There are people who love
what you do.
Others will always hate
what you do.

The majority have no idea.

Those are the souls
I observe on sidewalks
and in restaurants.
They are confused, angry, lost.
They stumble beautifully
through the fire.

Unknown Source

Sometimes the sadness
comes like a sucker punch
to the back of the head.
The assailant disappears
into the crowded street,
and we are stuck
nursing a painful wound,
never really knowing
its reason or cause.

Force for Good

Do not confuse forced civility
with human morality.
One is an aristocratic control.
The other protects the downtrodden.
Words and fists,
cocks and cunts,
they are the gifts of life.
Allow your heart to brim with cheer
and keep a sense of determination
nestled in your gut.

It's all in the knees

There are days
when the continuous beating
tempts us to lie on the ground
and give up the struggles
that make this ride matter.
I am begging you
to help each other
stand up
and fight together
until the end.

When the Hammers March

I rolled over in bed and you weren't there, baby. Alone. On the descent. It's the fourth or fifth drink when that vault door looks like it can be breached. The vault swells and begins to open with the natural beauty of a flower or a cunt ready to redefine the parameters. You want to enter the vault and swim in its thick truths, but you are afraid, so afraid of what will be found. It's funny how some memories are valued yet ghosts and demons are not allowed to exist. They do not fit the dress code, do they, baby? Standards are everything to the frightened child inside each of us.
Turn in the traitors.
Love the physically fit.
Scared or possibly sacred,
we tremble
in an orgasmic sensation
of masochistic satisfaction
as we stroke off sadistic bullies.
Independence is not part of the plan. All things are connected through time and space. Kill a fly, bring down a dictator on the other side of the planet fifty years ago. Have another drink. Think on this. Yes, six shots. Eight shots. Now you see, the rose petals and thorns siphon the blood and no one is there to save you, except the Wall. Just like mother, it will snuff out the world and then it will leave you for the crows. Build it in a circle, a tight cave of permissible thoughts. It must be tall and strong, very strong.
Poured concrete. Grandfather's steel.
Quivering inside the dark fortress,
you cannot pray or chant.
You forgot the words over the death bed
of the dying matriarch,
and you know what it is to be truly lost.
Take a break.

Whiskey and ginger ale are too much sugar.
Diet ginger ale has too many chemicals.
Diabetes must be avoided while toxic fictions are held close.
No more shots. The bottle feels good in the hand.
Feel the drink burn your temporary throat
of your temporary life.
That's right. Drink.
The stranglehold makes you want to lie down.
When fragile hammers march down Grant Street,
you must obey.
Do not weep, baby. The strongman will make you whole
for all time. In violence we trust. Be beautiful.
Practice your accepted words. Be a software wizard,
but not a witch or a bitch or a prick.
Happy proles live long lives breathing
filtered nitrogen-oxygen blends, unlike criminals,
the illegals who taste the soot of blue collar ancestors.
Fuck them, baby. The beatitudes are forgotten
and the golden calf has prevailed
in its total, absolute rule,
always and forever.
So I say to you in the moonlight,
this shit is the echo of an invisible laugh
from the darkness
of a long concrete hallway.
Have a drink.

Freedom Revealed

Laying on my back
in the alley,
drunk and sick,
I gazed at the blanket of stars.
The cosmos above revealed
itself as an endless sea
of lost hopes
and sacred prayers.
In that moment,
I was free.

Loser Lesson

I was once beaten
hard
by a large man
with red fire eyes
and froth on his lips.
Don’t worry, baby.
I gave as good
as I got.
That day, I learned
to survive.

Crack and Crumble

Those who speak truth
without fear
are the first to bleed
from hundreds of cuts
delivered by the sharp tongues
of wretched villains.
In suffering, truth tellers trudge on,
comforted only by history.
The next generation will listen.
Liars isolated in their torment
from cheap victories,
their mouths ooze the toxins
of lies that follow lies,
until the lies crack,
and, finally,
the lies crumble.

drop drop deluge

the pouring rain
much like venom or love
plunges toward the soil
without concern for anything
but its task to tumble and fall
until it is caught

the ground has no choice
no free will to deflect the rain
it must absorb the onslaught
of cold unyielding tears

eventually the soil overruns
from the rain's turmoil
shoulders slumped
back broken
its muddy remains
slide away

a new life
begins

Forethought

I stopped walking
and closed my eyes
in the middle of the sidewalk
during rush hour downtown.
The weak and the greedy
washed over me like a current
from a polluted river
filled with monotone voices
and hard-soled shoes.
The surrounding air
tasted of rancid meat.

Across the street,
a black man dressed in white
casually leaned against a wall.
He watched me in the crowd.

I believe he waited for me to leave,
so he could reveal his wings
among those who lacked vision,
and then he would fly away.

Gaze Through Bubbles

Three old women played cards
at a table next to me inside the café.
The new reading glasses gave me tunnel vision,
a pleasant bubble that shielded me
from reality while I banged away
at the typer and swilled cups of coffee.

Between hands, one of the women
said to me, "You're always in here writing."
"Yeah," I said. "That's probably true."
Another woman turned to face me.
"You must have a lot to say."
Her words sparked self-analysis.
"I don't have a lot to say, but I do have
much to escape."

The old women kind of nodded,
and then they went back to their game.
I took off the glasses for a minute
to gaze out the window.

Laugh at Forever

Sitting in a dim room
drunk on sweet bourbon
and consumed by hard memories
the surrounding air ignites
into a blanket of red fire
From a favorite chair we curse
the dead who wronged us in life
We murmur prayers for forgiveness
from gods we question
We spill tears onto the canvas
of the mind's perfect oil painting
that portrays all the lost years

After that poison is vomited
we laugh hard at forever
because there is no escape

A Break from Mayhem

Sitting at a picnic table
on the shore of the river,
the current swelled and ran
with brutal determination
while the wind howled.
One could feel the battle
between the elements
unfold in a cosmic struggle.

I opened my pocketknife
and stuck the tip of the blade
into the tabletop.
If the river called, I'd be ready
to spill my blood on behalf
of that great spirit.

The timbers of the table
had weakened over the years
from the endless war.
I spun the blade slowly
and watched strips
of its wood fibers cut away.
With time and patience,
I'd bore a permanent hole.
Instead, I folded the blade
and placed the knife in my pocket.
The struggle that awaited me
transpired elsewhere.

Heaven on Earth

Most people believe
Heaven on Earth
is hitting the lottery.
Give me
a full bottle of Jack,
the typer,
a soft chair,
and the imagination
of a wasted youth
that returns home
after a long exile.

I will then show you
Heaven on Earth.

Silent Withdrawal

Sometimes on Sunday mornings,
I'll awaken, take a leak, shut off the phone,
and then lay back in bed
for three more hours.
The world can't disturb you
under the covers. The cockroaches,
they always want meaningless conversations.
Scurrying around brunch buffets,
they wear good church clothes.
Their perfume and cologne reeks
of gossip, that longing for violence.
They must protect the small privileges
earned by turning a blind eye
to the murders of faceless souls.

Out on the streets, it's different.
Whores suffer withdrawal from a hard night
while bums drink free coffees
given by kindly café workers.
They stare at the pavement in silence,
their eyes transfixed on visions
of what could have been.

I stay in bed and stare at the ceiling
and think about the good times,
when we laughed at our troubles
until they were forgotten.

Exclusively You

For all the flaws
of the body, mind, and soul
we must carry through life,
I've never met a better man
or someone I'd rather be.
People who follow celebrity culture
breathe air laced with envy
of great beauty and great wealth.
I never understood
why anyone should give up
a unique life for a template.
They are them.
You are you.
I am me.

Scratch and Chat

Many years ago,
it was common to see a cat
sunning itself on a brick wall
or stretched out in the grass
on sunny afternoons.
Now cats are kept indoors,
away from the birds and the mice
and the long fingers of the mob.
I cannot speak for everyone,
but things felt a little better
when the cats were around.
Friendly ones would hop up
onto park benches
for a scratch and a chat.
Lonely souls made friends,
and madmen on sidewalks
were exposed to a love
they were otherwise deprived.

Standby Mode

I really don't know
how many glasses
of whiskey I've drained
or how many hours
I've stared out windows
while waiting
for the world to awaken
from its drunken slumber
and begin to improve.

Finish the Job

The people inside churches
and casinos and jails,
they all know death will come.
Some of them pray the reaper
will visit sooner rather than later.
Slick managers at the jobs,
the young in foggy night clubs,
and the parents at amusement parks,
their eyes reflect everlasting
life without age or disease.
Sitting on a bench next to the river,
I aggressively blew cigar smoke
in the reaper's face.
'Come on,' I whispered,
'finish the fucking job.'

every day

create art
every day
if you cannot
then make just one
piece of art
which is the work of life
make it imperfect
and worthy of memory
every day

Bosses say good morning
to remind us of the power
they died so many times to attain
Enthusiasm we display in the returned greeting
is to exhale a blackened piece of the soul
That part is sacrificed
not on a white marble altar
but on a cheap countertop
that will not exist in five years

Bones Across Rails

There are days, baby,
when I can almost understand
the sweet tinge
of the steel barrel's tip.

As a kid, I learned
about the sorry bastards
in the old days who jumped
off the Westinghouse bridge
onto the train tracks below.

I thought they were mad.

Now I realize, when the prison
goes on without pause
while the body succumbs to age,
the spirit cries for relief.

The men who splattered
their guts across the tracks,
they weren't mad.
Their bodies were the only tools
that remained to put a stop
to the very machines
that murdered their souls.

Know Thy Worth

Across the web and on TV,
we are told to seize the means
of our short lives.
Those same authors and celebrities,
they take gluttonous pleasure
in forbidding us to seize the means
of our own productions.
To live one's truth requires us
to throw off the mob's lies.
Anything less is a betrayal
to the very precious gift
we call life.

Fix it, don't bitch it

I don't believe
anyone should be blamed
for trying to make it.
So many are offended
if a man sells drugs
or if a woman sells ass.
It takes courage
to truly live free.
Perhaps the offended
are lost in regret
for choosing to serve
a system of power.

Grasp and Pull

When the proles see in reds,
the rich lose their heads.
Bathed in the blood of villains,
workers dance and laugh,
they fuck and love.
Whores are redeemed.
Books are embraced.
Drink is consumed.
The blue-green Earth,
after such a long abuse,
is finally reclaimed.

Poverty Soot

The sidewalks were covered in soot
in our urban town outside of Pittsburgh.
That shit got under our fingernails,
smeared on our clothing, and in our hair.
No one ever had any money,
except for the wives and mothers.
They kept dollar bills tucked away
in their bras, and only removed the stashes
for milk, chipped ham, and bread.
Sometimes a random old man
would pay us 50 cents to sweep his porch,
so he could pretend civility for a day
before the soot returned.

Crisis of Knowing

No one cared
about the existential threat.
The overweight men
with good city jobs
and standard suburban wives,
they watched sports
and drank beer.

I was the crazy one,
the madman on the corner
standing on his box,
screaming about rising seas.
'It's like the second coming!'
I'd scream in the hope
someone would smile
and grant me salvation.

Most people didn't listen.
Some grew annoyed.
They'd say, 'Go home, idiot.
We've heard enough.'
So, I'd walk off, alone, defeated.
A sandwich, a glass of bourbon,
and a night's rest gave me the energy
to scream again.

One day, a young woman sidled up.
'Why are you making waves?'

I climbed down off my box
and looked her in the eye.
'I know too much.

Now, I can't go back.‘
She shrugged her shoulders
and walked off. I figured
she'd done herself a favor.
‘Drink and be merry,‘ I whispered,
‘while you can.‘

Guided by the Muse

That friend inside the bar,
he told me to write a novel.
'Someday,' I said.
'How come not now?'
'The words gotta pour out of me.'
What I'd failed to mention then,
but I write now, is the words pour
when the stars align
within the cosmos of our minds.
Life is a gift. In our short time,
the words come in varying forms.
The writer is not in control
of those moments.
We are mere subjects
guided by the muse.

Red Pop

When dad took me to the Slovak Club,
the railroaders would drink drafts
and buy me glasses of red pop.
Those men smiled and called me friend.
They'd tell me, 'Always support workers,
the little guys, or else the companies
will murder you like a slave.'

Forty years later, their sons
type out vile hatred over smartphones
onto Facebook and Twitter.
They say, 'Kill the liberals
and the unions and the Muslims.
Don't let them breed.'

I think about the railroaders
from time to time.
I imagine they died alone
in great torment,
while their wives fucked villains
and their sons' souls
were drowned
in black pools of rage.

Bouquets and Sewage

Inside the suburban diner
an hour from dawn,
the people's drooped faces
reveal exhaustion,
the weariness of soldiers
who've smelled far too many
funeral home bouquets.

All they need is a little love
to shoot them over the moon.

One young man in a work jacket,
he sips coffee while staring
at the crease lines in his palm.
Those hands were made for sacrifice.
That's good because he's got nothing
else to offer up to the gods.
His lover is still asleep at home.
She is warm under the sheets.

He chuckles to himself.
Life can be a shit show,
but sometimes
swimming through sewage
has its rewards.

Fusion

Standing on the sidewalk,
it's fascinating to watch people
race to and from office buildings,
the tails of their jackets fluttering
in desperate breezes.
Through sheer will,
the imagination has the power
to slow everything down.
We can then dive deep
inside ourselves
for a moment of exploration.
Our guts are fusion reactors
where wisdom fuels truth.
The mind then rises
above the mob.

Labor Void

I was out of work
Money dried up fast
The gas bill doubled
The rent tripled
A friend offered his couch
but pride bit that feeding hand
I spent the days arguing
with blank walls
their vicious rebuttals
unveiled the vile truth of men
The nights were about cheap booze
constant trips to the pisser
poetry about soft lips until dawn
Anything to escape
the anxiety
the poverty
the disappointment
in myself

The next job pulled me out
of the misery
I then waited patiently
for it to return

Laugh and Starve

In our working lives,
we must wake up early,
wear clothes we loathe,
follow rules, and perform tasks
that make little or no sense.
My only objection to this slow death
is that we're robbed the freedom
to fuck a stranger at 2:27 PM on a Thursday.
We should lie on our backs atop gritty pavement
in the middle of a busy street and laugh
at the clouds that float aimlessly.
We should sit in dark rooms,
drunk on bathtub moonshine,
and watch the neighbors scratch their asses.
We should starve between meals
while the spirits haunt our memories
and transports us to new dimensions
of truth and madness.

In Waiting

Back in the small town,
we hung around the gas station
in the afternoons and at night.
We drank cartons of iced tea
and laughed about nothing.
We watched others live
the lives we wanted,
but weren't quite ready
to begin.

Fast Food Lunch

Inside the fast food joint
a woman stood behind the register
with frizzed hair and a stained uniform.
Her blank expression revealed defeat
after a lifetime of broken promises.

'I've been on my feet all day,'
she said, 'from the time I woke up
and got my kids ready for school.
I even stood on the bus.
Maybe I'll sit on the way home.'

I ordered a sandwich
and then drove back to the job.
Thoughts of that woman's soul
flashed through my mind
as I devoured each bite.

Steel Bars

On the construction site,
I dropped a shoulder of 2X4s.
While retrieving the planks,
I cursed the sky and the job.
An older guy barked at me,
'This shit's better than jail.'
His wisdom taught me
there are two prisons:
one with and one without
visible steel bars.

No Fucks

A young woman in a retail uniform
leans against the wall
outside of a useless store
in a useless suburban town.
The woman cradles a cigarette
between two fingers.
She stares at the screen of a smartphone,
enjoying long, satisfying drags.
This woman pays no mind to the people
that walk by. They don't matter.
She's above it all, below it all,
a slave whose mind transcends
the limits of time and space.
The deep red color of her fingernails
and the black eye shadow tell me
a man once tried to own her.
Through struggle, she made it
to the other side, and now,
no one is permitted that close.
Her life outside the gig
is hers alone.

Masquerade

Half drunk on good bourbon
in a friend's living room,
my buddy chuckled in a kind of sadness,
that way we do when booze uncovers sins.
The guy told me he wears many masks
for different aspects of his life.
He has a mask for the job,
a mask for the wife, a mask for the kids.
The man has so many masks that their weight
often times crushes his soul.
They force him to hide from the world.
I told my friend to drop the masks
and instead to seek out his truth.
He told me the words are easy,
but the work of change is brutal.

At a job interview months later,
the boss asked if I was excited
to help the company 'achieve success.'
With a forked tongue, I feigned interest
about bartering away my flesh for cash.
In the car on the way home, my fingernails
began to rake over the side of my face.
I subconsciously scraped away
the plastic resin that had replaced
a once-authentic life.

Bound to Roam

Surrounded by buffoons
in my youth,
their simplistic views
made me the outcast.
Quietly despised, I endured
their hatred because I didn't know
there were others
who thought like me.

Books unveiled a larger world
with interesting people
who told amazing stories.
I wanted to be like them,
but early fatherhood held me down.
Instead, I used those bound pages
to unleash the mind.
Vivid dreams of flight over lakes
we usually lose with age
returned and grew potent.
Knowledge gave me insight,
power, understanding
of the land and the seas.

During the days,
I was imprisoned by fools.
When the sun went down,
I roamed free.

Choose the Chain

When one works a job,
the morning ritual
is to be reminded of the slavery.
One is chained to the boss,
the employer, the absence
of a free life.

When one does not work,
the morning is a void.
The chain still exists,
but it is bolted to nothingness.
Empty and without purpose,
one counts the passing days
as every part of life begins to empty.
The refrigerator, the bank account,
the list of women and friends,
it all goes bare
as the rent comes due.

The chains are burdens.
Both have their benefits
and both chafe the neck raw.
One must determine
which chain to carry
through our days.

Truthful Rejoinder

The poets in the digital age
hunger for constant approval.
As cowards, they hide in fear
behind the mob's outrage.
In a constant search for validation
within shallow mud puddles,
every penned word betrays
the pursuit of truth in art.
Lost in a fog of redactions,
I just don't know
if these poets will ever find
truth again.

Free Falling Fictions

I pissed away
so many dollars
on the pool tables.
The fantasy spoke to me.
It said, 'Keep going.
You'll be the next hustler,
a better Jackie Gleason.'
Of course, I lost more
than I'd ever won.

That's how it goes
when reality grows harsh
and its fangs plunge in.
The chimeric dreamscape
calls to us.
Its sweet temptation
is a sinkhole of slick mud
that swallows tormented souls,
whose smeared vision
impedes the necessary foothold
to ascend.

Grinch Dream

Down in the city streets,
young people danced.
They made sounds of joyous music
and called for a peaceful love,
the final farewell to arms.
I cursed them under my breath
from atop the corporate tower.
Enraged, I whispered,
'How dare they cheer?'

Sat upon the toilet
in the men's room,
I removed my car keys
and flipped through them
to find the most jagged key.

At first, the ridges felt good,
similar to a small massage pulled
across the fatty flesh of my thigh.
Pressing harder, the key cut deeper.
The pain matched the torment
inside my guts.
When the blood came,
I imagined vomiting up
the control placed upon me
by lesser men.

The blood trickled down
my calf, absorbed into the sock.
I then started a new cut
below the first.
A new stream trickled down

the other side of my calf.

I cupped my palm
under one of the streams.
Warm and soft, the blood
carried the only truth
I'd ever trusted.

As a tribal warrior
preparing for his death,
I smeared the blood
across my forehead,
my cheeks, my lips.

Out on the sidewalk,
the sunshine blinded
part of my vision.
The booming sounds of love
and laughter deafened me.
A thin young man or a boy
with a baby face approached.
'Are you hurt?'
I reached into my pants
to gather more blood.
With a fury, I then smeared it
upon him, to murder
his innocence.

'What are you doing?'
the boy said, his expression
disgusted by my truth.
A young girl ran into his arms.
She said, 'He is too far gone
to save. Leave him.'

I then fell to my knees
and wept
alone
in exile of touch,
divorced of sight,
and removed
from that joyous music
until black.

Tick, tick, tick...

Behind the walls of a suburban office,
people dressed in slacks and skirts
have these dark crescent moons
under their eyes.
A woman walks urgently
from her desk to another woman's desk.
Her entire face is coated in makeup.
Still, the crescents bleed through
as an act of rebellion to the conditioning.
A man in a wrinkled gray shirt,
he talks to another man in cheap shoes.
They discuss hunting and guns.
Every time the men fantasize out loud
about shooting deer or terrorists,
they exhale deep and sit back.
Their voices rise in delight.
So many others sit quiet in their cubicles,
yet their torment is deafening.
Countless silent screams go on and on.
They will not dissipate.

212° Fahrenheit

In the extreme fringes of civilization,
both the paupers and the tycoons
are afforded the freedom
to fuck their neighbors' wives
and wear desperation
as priceless jewels.
The responsible middle
in chain restaurants and churches,
offices and cafés,
their hands shiver
in a form of imprisoned terror.
One overheard howl at the moon
or a single misplaced orgasm,
and the mob finally has an excuse
to exorcise their repressed madness.
In a self-righteous fit of rage,
each sinner is destroyed.

My Arrogance

In real life
I'm the modest guy
who laughs at jokes
and fails at math trivia.
Sometimes I play the fool,
so others feel very good
about their insufferable
opinions, lies, insights.

I never tell them I'm a genius
who sees the world in colors
they are unable comprehend.
They wouldn't believe it
and then they'd abandon me
for their own kind.

They say geniuses are lonely,
forced to live in desperation.
While I prefer to be alone
with the ghosts and the demons,
my words must be read,
absorbed, understood.
I do not wish to feel
the absence of value.

Experts

If you seek an education,
go to a university
or a trade school.
If you want to learn,
talk to the bums, the whores,
the immigrants in fields.
They're the experts
on humanity.
Their wallets are as empty
as their stomachs,
but their souls
are dipped in gold.

Flying Bartender

I had a job interview today
over the phone,
with a man who didn't know
what he wanted
in a new employee.

When it ended, I sat on the back stoop.
A butterfly with blue wings came by
and landed on the step next to me.
It slowly moved its wings.

For the next five minutes,
I poured my heart out.
I vented the stress of poverty,
the violent onslaught of the bills.
The butterfly listened,
without talking over me,
nor did it feel the need
to offer pointless advice.

Once I'd emptied my guts,
my voice fell silent.
That butterfly then launched.
It flew in a couple of uneven circles
in front of my face
and then it flapped to the trees.
For a few brief minutes,
the grass and the leaves
appeared a little greener.
The sun felt a little warmer.
My mind swum in memories
of childhood laughs.

Tethered

On the sidewalk downtown,
a businessman stared out
into the sunny spring street,
his mind elsewhere.
He gripped a laptop
and a folder full of papers
while stealing a glimpse
of the world and the life
he no longer enjoyed.
The fantasy came to an end
once his smartphone rang.
The tether had tightened,
and so he returned
to his cage.

Chuckle Tears

A retired woman wrote to me.
She said, 'Your words helped me.
I watched my nephew murder
my husband. He also tried
to push me into his truck.
He was going to kill me too,
but the neighbors screamed
and they called the cops.'

The nephew was caught,
imprisoned, forgotten by all,
except for that retired woman.
For several years, she refused
to step outside or see friends.

'Your words made me remember
my truth,' she said. 'I go out to lunch
once a week with my friends now.
They're all widowed. You know
how it is with us old ladies.
I just wanted you to know
some of us are reading.'

I closed the email on the typer
and then stepped into the kitchen.
The whiskey bottle didn't feel right,
so I set it down. Palms flattened
atop the counter, tears rolled
and my breathing labored.
I wept for that woman.
After a moment passed,
I chuckled at the sunlight

that reflected bright
off of the white stovetop.

That day, I learned the only real beauty
lies within struggle.

Unearned Ejaculation Privileges

Once upon a time,
there was a local writing group
that met inside a chain coffee shop
to discuss writing mechanics.
A woman in a vest said,
'You must be educated to write
and you must write every day.'
The group then mocked
people who do not understand
the proper nuances
of punctuation or grammar.

I decided to add my voice.
'The best writers are slaves.
They build words of hard truths
when the fire comes
between jobs and between lovers.
Everything else is masturbation
without the payoff.'

The other writers stared down
at their shoes, except that woman.
She rolled her eyes
and then said something forgettable
about Sylvia Plath.

I quietly exited the coffee shop,
knowing I'd never attend
another writing group
ever again.

Starved Souls

On the used car lot,
it was my job to shine the cars
well beyond their worth
and muck out the sludge and phlegm
from the floor drains.
Both tasks were the toxins
that pollute men's souls.
The salesmen stared out windows
with their suicide eyes.
In thrift store suits,
they chain-smoked generic cigs
to break the boredom.
Upon that slab of suburban pavement,
we danced with demons
during the day
and lay starved atop soiled mattresses
through the night.

Big Time

Sitting in the café,
a writer said to me,
'I love coming here
to write on Saturdays.
I work hard in the week,
and this is my downtime.'

I got up from my seat,
tired, worn, quietly enraged.

'Did I say something wrong?'

I looked the writer square in the eye.
'You know the difference
between you and me?
I do this shit to eat
and because it's who I am.
You do it to pretend.'

The writer didn't respond.
I found a different seat,
and then stared at the typer,
unwilling and unable
to make the words.
At least sharing that truth
made me feel
big time.

Know When to Exit

Hauling drywall on a rural job site,
still a boy in most respects,
I looked around at the men.
Their faces and their hands
contained cracks,
the kinds of fractures
that form from age and neglect
often found in old pottery.

The job was their daily escape
from the halfway houses,
the bills, the women, the kids.
Some of the men were drunkards.
Others were drifters on the run.
Every man on the site murdered
me with his dead eyes.
They tasted my innocence
on gusts of the winter's wind.

One snowy afternoon,
the boss drove off for an errand.
The hammering and sawing stopped.
Silently, the men moved closer,
their dead eyes stared me down.
I'd be bloodied, robbed
of my tool belt and boots,
and then rolled into a ditch.
The odds were eight to one.
So, I walked off that job
and never returned.

Whispered Sins

I drank after the job
most nights, alone.
Those times were simpler,
even if they were filled with pain.
Friends believed I was lonely.
At least, that's what I told them
while secret demons kept me company
under each phase of the moon.
Night after night, they whispered
evil reminders of my past back at me.
I tried to drown the demons,
but their voices kept hissing.

As the years went on, I learned
to accept things for what they are.
The demon whispers then faded
and, eventually, they slithered
back into the darkness.
Alone with a new confidence,
that's when the claims of loneliness
finally became my truth.

Click, Click, Click

I have this large folding knife.
Sometimes, I flip the blade open
until the lock clicks.
I do this over and over and over.
I tell the annoyed and the frightened
the click of the lock
makes a satisfying sound.
That's half true.
It's the blade that really turns me on.
The blade's edge is the thin present
that whittles historical remnants
from a possible future.
A man understands thirst
when the glass runs dry.
He knows his limits
when cold steel is pressed
against his flesh.

See in Colors

The cynics see rapists
around every dark corner.
The bohemians feel love
cascade down to the sidewalk
from every balcony.
The artists and the poets,
we see colors radiate
as heat and sex and violence
from those who pass by
our wooden stools.
Our visions are stroked
onto paper in unending battles
to hold off the demons of madness.
Those demons find their way
into every piece of work
only we can see.

Wisdom Cometh

On an early spring evening,
a beautiful man jogged
on a new city sidewalk
under a clear blue sky.
His hair had stylish waves.
He worn designer sweats
and clean sneakers.
That man ran and breathed
in a straight rhythmic line.
His body never leaned.
He never lost balance.
I imagined that beautiful man
worked in a clean office.
He'd perfected small talk.
He fucked his women
on a clean bed
inside a swank apartment.
That man had no dreams,
but to keep jogging
and hang on to youth
until wisdom finally comes
and informs him of truth,
that he'd better learn
to zig and to zag.

The Snatch Life

Murderers and thieves
lurk around every corner.
The honest ones use weapons
to get what they want.
The others allow selfishness
to slowly manipulate weak men
into the madness of poverty.
All remaining strength
sapped away, the defeated
pray for death.

Asked, Answered

The barista in the café
said, 'You're always in here
writing and reading alone.
Why do you write?'
I paid for the coffee.
'Because I have to.'
'Why do you have to?'
'Words are power,' I said.
'Stories make people immortal,
and I've lost too many
friends and family members.'
The barista wiped the counter.
I walked back to the table,
drank the coffee, and made
more immortal words.

$20 Chili

I often make chili
when I'm broke.
The ingredients are $20
and I can get 5 meals
out of one pot.

Men and women I know
say, 'Seriously, again?'
In the past I've replied,
'It's delicious.'
Now, I don't bother
to respond.
There's no point.

They have lovers
to pay their bills
and buy them
pretty things.
When the relationships
no longer work,
they go to
families and friends
for support.

I no longer resent
their privileges.
I did when I was young,
scraping through soot
to make it
with a child,
insane mother,
sadistic bosses.

That was before
wisdom,
before I knew
how to make $20 chili.
It simmers
while piano music
plays softly
in the other room.

The same old scents
of surrender
and tomatoes
never change.
Aging idleness
makes me laugh mad
into the steel sink.
I do it for the echo.
I like the echo.
It proves
I am still here
for now.

Be Upright

Keep your back straight
when walking in the rain.
You'll have a better view
of the frightened rats
who scurry for the salvation
you've already found
within yourself.

Commune

Sitting on the cellar steps,
it was difficult to not admire
the rainwater that flowed
with determination across the floor.
Powerless to stop the flood,
I made a choice
to enjoy the fresh perspective.
So many others made feeble attempts
to control the inevitable
with sandbags and prayers.
I took a hit of whiskey
and then communed
with the storm.

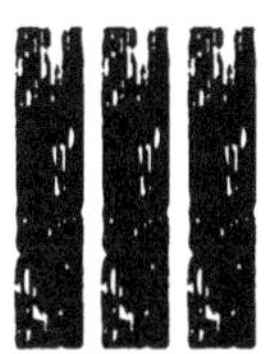

In the gentle rain
intimacy is fluid and easy
But one must be prepared
for flash floods and mud-cracking droughts
While the timid collapse
at first glance of a wilted flower
the courageous spirit
gives celebration to such hazards.
They challenge and enhance
the bonds that define us

Free Souls

The lovers and the fighters
both know that bitter
sweet tinge of struggle.
They are also the free souls
who deliver truth and emotion
upon apathetic servants.
Adorned in empty gray suits,
the mob lives only to criticize
those who rise above
the mundane.

Blank Canvas

She and I sat on the sofa
together.
She didn't speak,
her face a blank canvas.
I stared at the rounded folds
of the curtains
in thick silence.

The sadness that night
was something went wrong
and I just didn't have
the desire
to figure it out
or fix it.

It adds definition

Sidewalks and lovers
grow discolored
from unsuspected joys,
tormenting stampedes,
and the spilled blood
they endure.
It happens slowly
over time.

Punkdos

When I was young,
only the courageous
women colored their hair
pink or green.
They risked job security
and they ignored
the conformed standards.
That strength of spirit
turned me on
far more than tits or legs.
That hair is now mainstream,
so I pretend courage
is mainstream.

Death by Stink

Old lady perfume
wafts through the café.
The smell of wildflowers
rolled through baby powder
baffles me. That scent
is an asexual surrender
of life and love.
That stink is the active murder
of the will to go on.
It is malevolence
in the wind.

No Love Today

...from behind the counter,
she smiled at me in a deeper way.
Her eyes told stories
about ecstasy and the prison
of family life.
So, I went back to the table,
drank the coffee,
and I tried to exorcise
the temptations
through words.
The typer has always been
my most loyal lover.

Scorched

I've grown so tired
of hating you,
but I've hated you so long,
it's all I know.
After the foul odor of death fades,
fresh air will replace
that which we cannot change.
Staring out the window,
my chest tightens from dread.
The pollution we've spewed
may have scorched the soil
where new trees must grow.

Keep Pumping

I may never understand
you. For certain,
you will never understand
me. That's okay.
It's the mystery, baby,
that keeps the heart pumping.
I can't think of another reason
to allow the blood to remain
in my veins.

Rust Lines

Atop the hillside,
she and I looked down
at the steel mill.
'The dirt is so black up here,'
she said, her voice confused.
I didn't have the energy
to tell her we stood on soot,
the particulates of coal and ore.
Some men visit graveyards.
I stand on the remnants of history
and look down onto the rust,
the bloody labor
of family.

It's Enough

The old woman hung around the café
most days, just to get away.
She wore her coat in the summer
and added a hat in the winter.
Her voice quivered
when she said her husband is dead.
She now lives with the kids.
They won't let her buy books.
She has too many books
about love and cooking and artists.
The old woman's husband loved books,
but now he's dead, and the kids,
they say it's enough.

Breathe, Struggle, Live

In the pursuit of truth
and justice and growth,
we cannot celebrate our angels
without acknowledging our demons.
Each of us are flawed humans.
We are magnificent disasters.
In our mutual struggles to breathe
and survive a mad world,
every step we take
and every word we speak
is a work of art.

Scratched and Dented

When the bathwater flows
over our heads and shoulders,
many of us believe
we are cleansed.
While that might be true
for the body,
a fraction of us hold a truth
that our sins and our virtues
are not easily washed away.
A handful of us grin
and wink at the demons.
The stains in our scratched
and dented souls feel right.
We prefer it that way.

Slowly Enclosed

Hundreds of years ago,
when people had visions,
the mob would gather
to say the visionary was touched
by God's grace.

Now, one dare not admit
any visions, for fear
their minds will be locked away.
'They are unclean!' the mobs scream.
The goal is an acceptable class
of artificial humans
who build artificial wares
with artificial intelligence.

Geniuses tell us artificials
will someday censor our words,
our thoughts and perspectives,
and destroy unique lives.
The geniuses must be blind,
because the first murders
have already happened
and they continue.

myself

I've met many men on sidewalks,
at jobs, in bars and cafés.
Some of these men held
strong principles.
Others sold their minds
and their bodies long ago,
usually to rather low bidders.
Of all these men of youth and age,
colors and religions,
I still prefer my own company
the most.

Perfect Waste

A guy in a suit at the bar
cracked an unfunny joke.
It was the kind of joke
only office drones understand
or find amusing.
His buddy spit out his whiskey
from the involuntary chuckle.
The guy said, 'Hey, man,
you're wasting perfectly good scotch.'
I thought the joke was a waste
of perfectly good words.

Breathe It Out

Are you awake?
Yeah, me too.
It's 2:30 AM.
I get it, baby.
Just breathe.
Breathe again.
Keep breathing.
Pay close attention
to each breath.
Breathing is what matters.
Keep breathing.
You'll get there.

Throat Scars

When we hit the whiskey,
we felt very good
for too short of a time.
The cowards and the whores
didn't disappear into the night.
At least their filthy claws
couldn't get a grip
on our throats.

Thick Hair

There was once a woman
with thick blonde hair that traveled
halfway down her back.
I loved that hair.
When I stroked it
or massaged her scalp,
that dame purred.

After a couple of meet ups,
she let me rape her
in the missionary position.
I reached under her back
and grabbed hold of that hair.
Her purrs only grew louder
as I fucked her hard, stabbing
in and out, over and over.
For a moment, she had become
my arch nemesis.

After a few minutes, I pulled out
and came over her stomach.
'Why'd you do that?' she said.
I didn't have an answer.
As I rolled over onto the bed,
her hair no longer interested me.
I faked it for a while
to be kind.
But it was time to move on,
and she knew it.

I think she's married now.

Over the Fence

‘At this point in my life,’
I said to the neighbor,
‘I can't think of a good reason
to not be drunk most of the time.’
Sly chuckled at my words,
but didn't have a response.
He then vented frustration
about his woman
and some video game.
I listened for a while,
until the glass went dry.
Then I walked inside
for a refill.

Hardship and Hope

Over an old gas stove,
Gram labored in the heat.
She fried potato pancakes
and boiled cabbage.
I sat at the table to watch her
perform that delicious magic.
Gram worked to feed us
day and night,
because love never stops.
'I step onto the back porch
when it's too much,' she said.
'No one sees me sweat.'
To the common observer,
her eyes conveyed hardship.
I saw hope.

Tearing Flesh

Con men make fools of us all.
Driven to the brink
of rage-fueled madness,
we must destroy the beauty
others hold dear.
Lovers, saints, children,
they all must suffer
long vengeful falls
against jagged teeth
of endless bloody chomps.
Nothing will save us,
but one day,
a rebirth will come
that resets the clock.

Locate the Blood

The coward trembles
when confronted
with the betrayal
of his brothers and himself.
He sweats fear
as he awaits retribution.
When the heat of rage
scorches his jaw,
the coward is left on the concrete
to rot alone in self-loathing.

The man who runs his mouth
like a whore,
he can at least bleed
like a man.

Eternal Affair

Of all human love affairs,
death is the greatest by far.
Most people dwell
on its madness in bed.
We form religions to explain it
and spend our precious years
trying to outrun it.
Out on the streets,
there are too many who take
immense pleasure
in thrusting death
upon others.

Everyone thirsts for eternal love.
No matter how hard we try
to find it in our lives,
each of us eventually finds love
within the cool embrace
of death's seductive charms.

Baptism Observed

A younger man with a backpack
hobbled down the bike trail
and then made his way
toward the riverbank.
He wore these pants
stained from oil,
scuffed from pavement.
His boots told stories
of rambling rejection.
His demeanor sung slow
cigarette songs
of sorrow.

Without hesitation,
that bum covered in filth
stepped into the water,
submerging those shoes
and the cuffs of his pants.
He then retrieved an old
water bottle from his pack
and plunged it into the river.
As an infant child cradled
over the brass basin,
that young spirit tilted backward
and then poured the water
over his head.

When a man has nothing,
that's the only time in his life
he can let go of the struggle
and begin anew.

Genuinely Lost

The rain always comes
at the most inconvenient times.
To those of us with open eyes,
each drop falls as a tear
to remind us of our grief
when we most need the sun.
Others use rainy days
as an excuse to hide from the pain
of facing their truths.

Without the inspiration to thrive,
the woke and the asleep
immerse ourselves in distractions,
easy escapes of cheap entertainment.
We forget every genuine thing,
every genuine friend,
and the reality that once defined
the most genuine stories
of our small lives.

Loving It

As a young man,
mentors and parents
told me over and over,
there's little money
in writing.
They didn't understand.
Words, much like truth,
are a lifelong pursuit.
So, here I sit
in a ramshackle house,
pouring blood on the typer,
loving every word
and every reader
that passes by.

Modern Politics

Branded as degenerates,
hated by the masses,
the broken and the abandoned
weep in whispered prayers.
These angels of truth are hidden
in dark back alleys
while false prophets
under synthetic lights
revel in artificial glory.
In a mania of hope,
the masses then destroy
the angels of truth
for the splendor
of victory.

The Maxim

The writer's job
is to build the words,
not perform for applause
or join cheap cliques.
The printed word, baby,
that's the nervous anticipation
for the 300 pound whore
who sucks the best cock.
Words are the hit of whiskey
after the sun drops
below the buildings.

Better Entertainment

We were at the ballgame
in the cheap seats,
almost 90 degrees in May.
Hardly anyone sat near us,
except this young couple.
They argued and bickered
about former lovers, cars, bills,
throughout the entire game.
The woman had good tits
and hair and hips.
He didn't have much,
just a thin mustache
and very few hairs
blotched across his legs.

That couple proved more fun
than the ballgame.
I stared at them for over an hour.
Eventually, the woman had enough
of her man's backtalk. 'You're a cheater
with a small dick!' she screamed.
Wagging her finger in his face,
she gave it to him
good and strong.

When that dame stood
to better articulate
the disappointment
she clearly held inside
her own flawed heart,
the entire stadium broke
into applause.

Most of the people pretended
to applaud for a player's
diving catch of a line drive ball.
The honest ones,
we knew better.

Slide, Baby

If you can't spit fire,
swallow hard,
and then slide out of the way.
Words and time
are far too valuable
to be wasted
by the amateurs
of life.

The Gist

The value of food
is completely unknown
until the hunger sets in.
I can say the same
for love.

Free Moments

His positive spirit
made me feel free.
I breathed and dreamed.
Laughs came from the belly.
He wore leather work shoes
to the job, never boots.
But he loved cheap sneakers
and he wore them often.
When he was gone,
I no longer felt free.
So, it became important
to create a positive spirit
that would help others
feel free.

Reinvent

Our parents invented us
by reinventing themselves.
They threw away innocence
to reach the next stage.
Simple gratification,
that taste of life's bourbon,
forces a reinvention
of the mind and the body.
The soul thirsts for inspiration,
which means surrendering
the security of the mundane.
Always on the move, we must
seek knowledge and dreams.
We must reinvent ourselves
and what we choose
to love and to loathe.

The Smart Void

I often wonder what there is
to give, when there's no love
that remains in the gut.
If we cannot give love,
all things become dust
molded into pleasing shapes.

Inside the café, it is quiet.
The city and the maniacs
are forbidden from entering.
Inside, the regular people
with jobs and friends,
they read books by dead madmen
and drink expensive coffees.
From a distance of time and space,
they enjoy psychopaths whose hearts
once spilled over with love and rage.

The regular people are smart.
They know better than to love.
It's far safer to keep the world
behind the plate glass
and drink expensive coffees
and read mad words
to fill the void.

It's on the wind...

When the poetry doesn't work,
don't sweat it.
Get up from the chair
and go for a walk,
pet a strange cat,
befriend a blind man
on the sidewalk.
Few items are made of paper,
and the best poetry
is not printed on it.

Something Else

The guy who wore a scarf at the bar,
he chose not to write
because he's 'no Hemingway.'
I told him no one stops me.
Memories of Ginsberg, Frost, Thomas,
and even Bukowski's drunken ghost
make me feel at home in my words.
That didn't change the guy's mind,
so I told him to drink up
and do something else.

Fan Fiction

A guy wearing a sports jacket
pulled out a fat money clip
to pay for his drink.
He said to the bartender,
'I've died too many times.'
The bartender said,
'Tough out there?'
'You better believe it.'
'How many more lives
do you have?'
The guy exhaled.
'I don't know.'

When the privileged
turn real suffering
into a Saturday night fad,
those who scrape
truly are screwed.

Scream into the void

I've always enjoyed politics,
but I loathe people
who fight over the obvious.
That may be a contradiction.

I don't see it that way.

Politics isn't about solutions,
but rather specific emotions
geared toward morality
and our place in the world.

The seething rage
breathed through our teeth
and the warm embrace
of solidarity felt in our chests
cannot be expressed
at any other time
or in any other place.

After we've slobbered
upon our choices and ripped
into the souls of enemies,
we lie down on the mattress.
Exhausted from the fight,
we stare into the abyss
and wonder what hot hell
tomorrow will bring.

Vacuum

You have more power
than you realize
The problem is
you're more worried
about gossip
and hatred of neighbors
Therefore you stay apart
and never come together
That power is lost

Quiet Satisfaction

Sometimes we crush a bug
in self-defense.
Other times we crush bugs
in annoyance.
However, there are times
when we go out of the way
to step upon a lesser lifeform.
Such domination arouses
a sadistic pleasure
we cannot savor or even admit to
in civilized society.

future poem

my friends are dead
after all the years
together
they are gone
i am too damn old
to make new friends

what is the point
really
there is no reason

much like the pool cue
that sits in a corner
of the basement
i too know what it is
to be alone

friends are for
sharing news
and for fighting
over women

now there is no news
and the women
have vanished

it is time to sit
quiet and remember
the fast times
every once in a while
when some wisdom is imparted
to the young

Goodnight, Friend

In life, you brought laughs
and relief in tense moments.
You traded me tobacco
for booze and friendship.
You died this week. I'm sad
for the loss, but I have not wept.
I still hear the humorous timber
of your voice, and I remember
the way you let things slide.
That's your gift. The memories
of our chuckles together
dissolved the tears
before they could come.

Surrendered Spirit

I suffered you in life.
Some days included laughs.
Most days were fraught with venom
from the depression and torment,
that ruthless rage.
It wasn't until you died that I realized
I still love you.
Every single day,
your memory resurfaces.
I hold those good days close
and keep the bad days distant.
They're stored behind a frosted window,
so that I may access the moments,
yet not relive the pain.

Now that I've worked this out,
I surrender you.
Goodbye.

Hurtling

The passage of time,
that's the one war
everyone must wage.
It's also the one war
everyone will lose.
Take heart in the battles,
the small victories
that square your shoulders
and straighten your cock.
Those are the memories
of joy and splendor
we take to the end.

Run Currents, Run

I was born in a room
on a triangle of land and soot
between three rivers.
Just like the rivers,
I've been running
toward the fire
and from the smoke
all my days.
I'll let you know
when I make it.

left of me

...and
when death comes,
the grim reaper
will look down
at the thin tracing paper
of my soul.
slowly, he will reach out
for my emaciated remains,
but his bony fingers
will shred through me,
unable to grab hold.

confused, he'll ask,
'what is this?'
and i will answer,
'it's all they left of me.'

from under his black hood,
the reaper will blow
a gentle cool breeze
that floats my ravaged soul
into a velvet-lined sack.
without fears or regrets
and with all sins forgiven,
we will ride
over rolling hills
into eternity.

To despair is natural
Giving up is not
Hold out your hand
Someone is on the way
Nothing is over
until it's over
The next round
is about to begin

About the Author

Ron Gavalik is a writer
in Pittsburgh, Pennsylvania.
You can stalk him online.
He likes whiskey.

www.ingramcontent.com/pod-product-compliance
Lightning Source LLC
LaVergne TN
LVHW010620100826
845148LV00014B/3046

* 9 7 8 1 7 3 2 0 6 9 7 8 7 *